The Guide to Colorado Wineries

By Alta and Brad Smith

ISBN 0-9660149-0-1

Cover design: Mary DeSimone
Front Cover photographs by Brad Smith copyright 1997. Cover is a composite of two photographs: Vineyard is the Terror Creek Winery vineyard near Paonia. Mountains are the Elk Mountains behind Marble, Colorado.
Maps provided by Colorado Wine Industry Development Board and altered to fit the format of the book.
The information in The Guide to Colorado Wineries is accurate as of August 1997. However, prices, hours of operation, phone numbers, availability of wines and other items can change.
Printed in the United States of America by Johnson Printing Company, Boulder, Colorado

Acknowledgements

The authors owe a great deal to the many people who have helped — and encouraged — us. First, all the owners and winemakers at Colorado's wineries, who gave so generously of their time and were so patient in answering our questions. Also John Lowey, executive director of the Colorado Wine Industry Development Board, who went out of his way to provide help, open doors and track down information. Amy Nuernberg of Pyramid Printing Inc. in Grand Junction was instrumental in getting us the wine country maps and provided valuable advice. Also multi-thanks to graphic artist Mary DeSimone of Denver, who not only designed the cover, but also provided generous guidance in helping layout the book.

Authors' Note: None of the wineries paid to be included in this book.

Contents

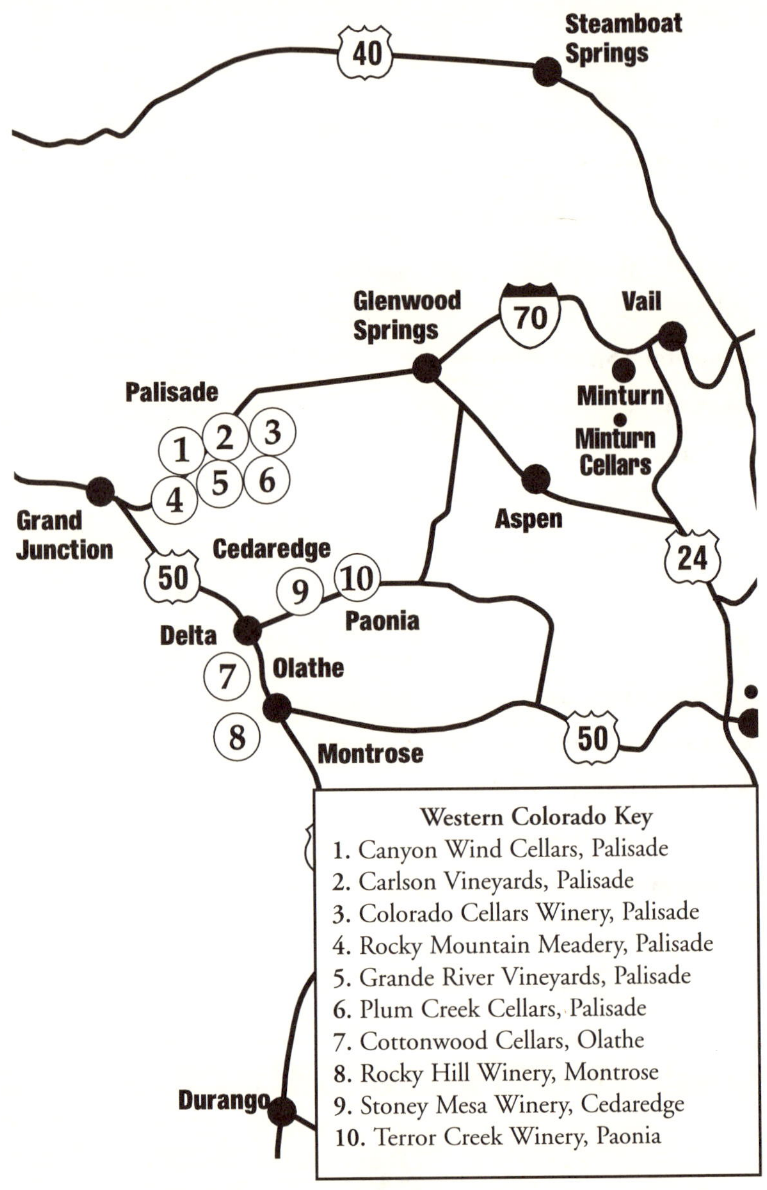

Western Colorado Key

1. Canyon Wind Cellars, Palisade
2. Carlson Vineyards, Palisade
3. Colorado Cellars Winery, Palisade
4. Rocky Mountain Meadery, Palisade
5. Grande River Vineyards, Palisade
6. Plum Creek Cellars, Palisade
7. Cottonwood Cellars, Olathe
8. Rocky Hill Winery, Montrose
9. Stoney Mesa Winery, Cedaredge
10. Terror Creek Winery, Paonia

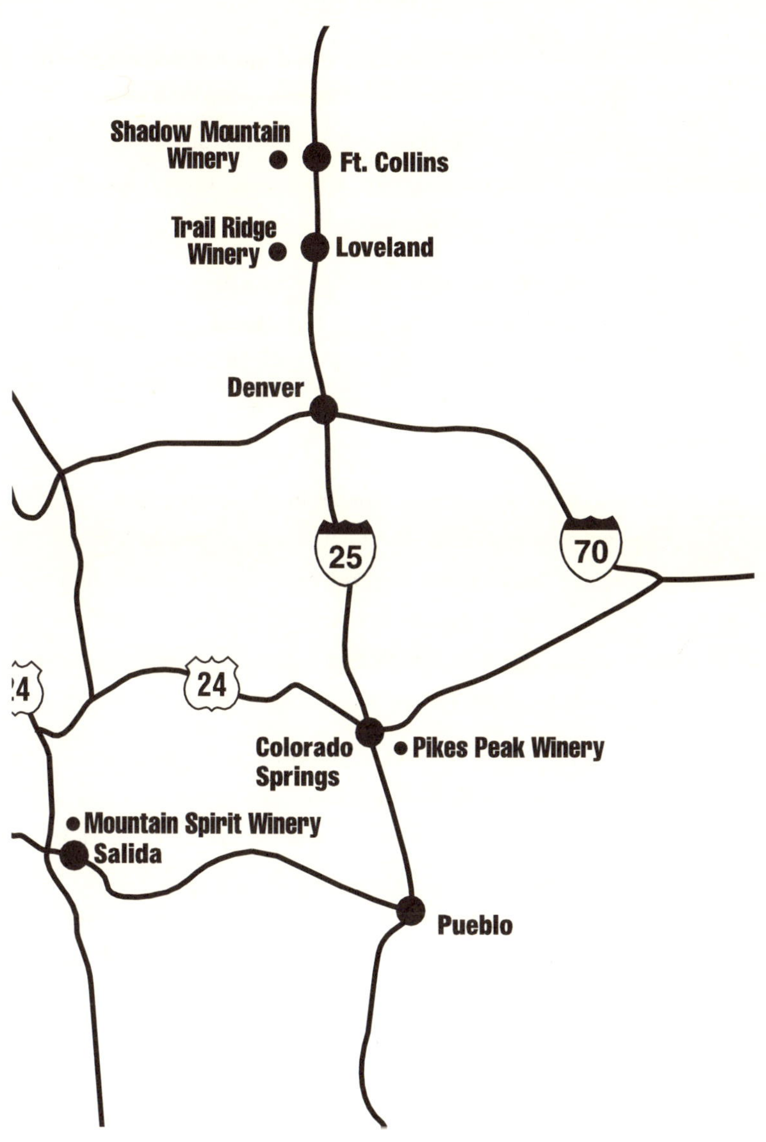
Shadow Mountain
Winery
Ft. Collins
Trail Ridge
Winery
Loveland
Denver
25
70
24
Colorado
Springs
Pikes Peak Winery
Mountain Spirit Winery
Salida
Pueblo

Introduction

There's one decided benefit about tasting and buying wine where it is made. That's especially true if you're also buying it from the person who made it. When you take the bottle home, or search it out at your local retailer, you also have the memory of where the wine came from. With each glass you drink, it's like returning to the winery.

Doing the research for this book was a joyous experience for the authors, and we think your own research can be just as much fun. Each of Colorado's wineries is distinct, and distinctive. As Colorado's wine industry matures, it is developing its own character generally, but each one retains its own personality.

If you are an old hand at visiting wineries in other states, as well as wine-tasting, you know what you're looking for when you walk in the door of a winery. If you're new to this, remember our No. 1 rule of wine-tasting — you're the best judge of what you like. The quality of Colorado wines may surprise those who haven't tried them. Don't pre-judge a wine by its name or label, or even by how the winery looks.

The authors don't pretend to be wine experts, knowing only what we like. For that reason you won't see any of our own ratings or preferences in this book. We didn't want to influence your choices, or your enjoyment. We did try to give you an idea of what the "experts" think by noting award-winners in the list of wines for each winery. If you're interested in learning more about these, ask the individual wineries and they can give you a list of their award-winners and where the awards were won. Also ask where you can buy their wines, and if they will ship them to you.

Speaking of awards, here's another one of our wine-tasting rules — just because the wine didn't win an award doesn't mean it isn't good. Some of the authors' favorite wines have won no awards for the simple reason the winery did not enter them in a contest.

In the back of the book is a short glossary of terms for those who want to know more about words used to describe wine. But you don't need to know these words to know what you like, and don't be intimidated by those who do speak "wine talk." If you want to explore this world further, there are numerous wine books explaining the intricacies of winemaking and wine-tasting.

Colorado Wine History

People have been making wine in Colorado more than 100 years. Then, as now, the grapes primarily were grown in the Grand Valley area along the Colorado River near Grand Junction. In 1899 the U.S. Census said Colorado produced 586,300 pounds of grapes and made 1,744 gallons of wine. Among the early growers was Gov. George Crawford, who had 60 acres of grapes and other fruit near Palisade.

Prohibition ended Colorado's small wine industry in 1916, when the state legislature enacted a prohibition statute four years before the country. Grape vines were ripped out of the soil across the state. Even though prohibition ended in 1933 with the repeal of the 18th Amendment, Colorado's wine industry lay dormant until 1968. That was the year that Gerald Ivancie established a winery under his name and planted premium wine grapes in the Grand Valley.

Six years later the Orchard Mesa Research Center opened, operated by Colorado State University, and has become a leading source of information about high-altitude viticulture. In 1977, the Colorado Legislature enacted a law granting special permits to small farm wineries, followed in 1990 with an act creating the Colorado Wine Industry Development Board.

The oldest existing winery opened in 1978 at Palisade, originally named Colorado Mountain Vineyards and then renamed Colorado Cellars. It was followed by Pikes Peak Vineyards in 1983, Plum Creek Cellars in 1985, Carlson Vineyards in 1988 and Grande River Vineyards in 1990. In 1990, the Grand Valley was designated a federal viticultural area.

There has been a mini-explosion of vineyards and wineries in Colorado since 1990. CSU research viticulturalist Richard Hamman Jr. noted in his 1996 "Colorado Grape Growers' Guide" that vineyard acreage increased from 242 to more than 400 acres over a five-year period and the number of wineries increased from five to fifteen.

In 1997 there were sixteen wineries, with at least three new ones on the drawing board. As we were going to press new wineries were preparing to open in Evergreen southwest of Denver and in Fruita, west of Grand Junction. Another was being planned in Boulder County. Unfortunately, one of the state's wineries, Columbine Cellars in Denver, stopped producing and its respected winemaker, Matt Cookson, moved to California.

Here are some facts that show the growth of Colorado's industry from 1990 to 1996, provided by the Colorado Wine Industry Development Board:

• There was a 220 percent increase in the number of wineries, from five to 16.

• A 300 percent increase in production capacity, to 208,500 gallons.

• An 82 percent increase in the acreage for wine grapes, to 440 acres. About three-fourths of those acres are in Mesa County, with 22 percent in Delta County.

• A 256 percent increase in the sale of wine from 1990 to 1996, to 223,440 liters, with a retail value of $4.5 million. Sales increased 58 percent in one year, from 1994 to 1995, which was a record year for production.

Distinctive Wines

Colorado has the distinction of having some of the world's highest wineries. One, Terror Creek Winery near Paonia, may be the highest in the world at 6,400 feet elevation.

This altitude, as well as Colorado's geographic location, give the state's wines some distinctive qualities. It also limits the kinds of grapes that can be grown to those that mature relatively early and are winter hardy.

Happily, two of the grape varieties that grow well in Colorado also are two of the most popular — chardonnay and merlot. About one-third of Colorado's vineyard acres are planted with chardonnay, with 18 percent in merlot. Following those in acreage are cabernet sauvignon (10 percent), pinot noir (8), cabernet franc and riesling (7 each), and gewurztraminer and sauvignon blanc (4), according to the 1995 CSU grower survey.

Viticulturalist Hamman says Colorado's intense sunlight and cool nights combine to make the grapes high in acid content as well as color. Acid gives wines a distinctly crisp taste that most people enjoy. "Grapes that survive Colorado winters can mature and produce fruit with highly desirable oenological (wine making) characteristics," Hamman said in his 1996 growers guide.

Colorado wines have a growing reputation, both inside and outside the state's borders.

A 1996 consumer survey showed Colorado residents had increased their consumption of the state's wines by 37 percent since 1992. More than half those surveyed said they were "very satisfied" with Colorado wines and 73 percent of those who had tasted Colorado wines said they very very likely to buy more.

Colorado wines have done well in blind tastings with wines from other states. In 1994, Colorado wines outscored their California rivals (from such vintners as Kenwood, Robert Mondavi, Buena Vista and J. Lohr) by a score of 398-to-369 and won half of the wine pairings. Colorado wines didn't fare as well in a similar blind tasting with Texas wines, winning just two of the eight pairings.

There also are anecdotes about sommeliers (certified wine experts) who have confused some Colorado wines with premium wines of Europe.

Although there is healthy competition among the wineries, most recognize the need to build the state's industry as a whole. "A lot of work goes into building the industry," says Grande River Vineyards owner Stephen Smith. "You need to be part of something bigger, not just yourself."

Most experts believe that if Colorado's wine industry is indeed going to continue to grow, it needs to do so because of its own distinctive qualities and not because it is trying to emulate California or some other state. As Colorado residents continue to discover these qualities, the word will spread.

Besides visiting the winery, one of the best ways to explore Colorado wines is through festivals and wine-tastings. We've included a list of some of the more popular ones in the back of the book. One that features most state wines is the Colorado Mountain Winefest in Palisade held on the third weekend of September.

We think visiting the winery itself is the best discovery of all and invite you to take the adventure yourself. Good hunting and good tasting!

Front Range Wineries

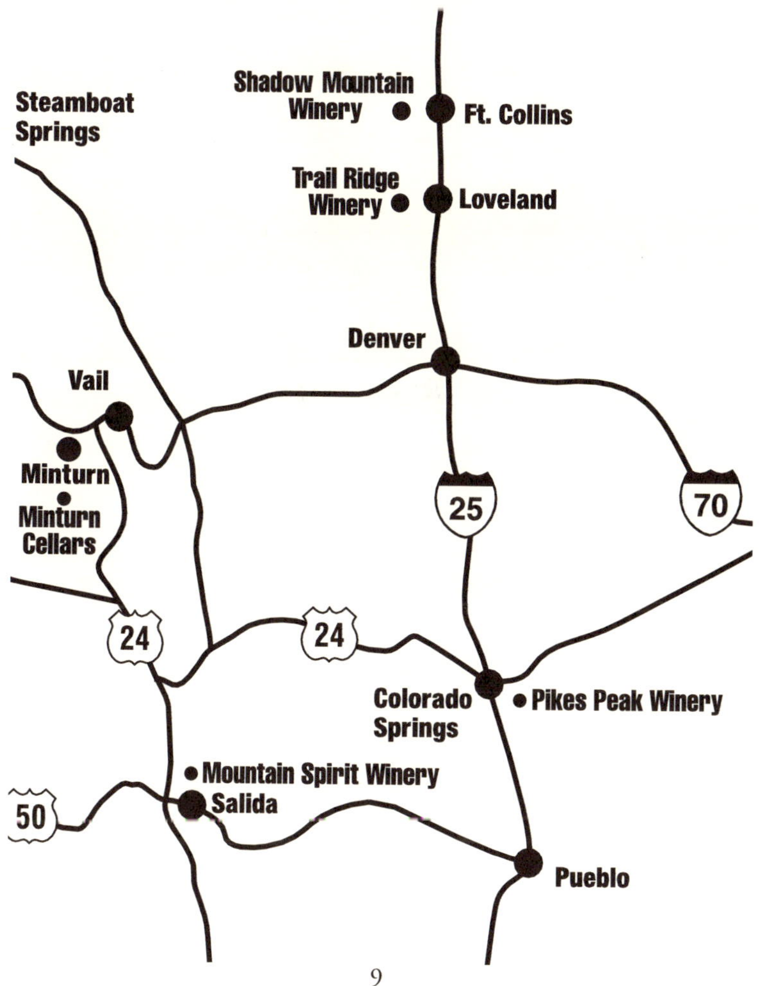

Trail Ridge Winery

Owners: Tim Merrick, Mark Fiore, Ron Binz, Wes Melander, Howard Golden
Winemaker: Tim Merrick
Year founded : 1994/licensed 1995
Address: 4113 W. Eisenhower Blvd., U. S. 34, Loveland, CO 80537
Telephone: 970-635-0949
Tasting room/ store hours: Summer hours: 12 p.m. to 5 p.m. daily, Spring/Fall: 12 p.m. to 5 p.m. Saturday and Sunday; closed January, February, and March.
Price range of wines sold at the winery: $5.00 to $16.00
Directions: Located on U.S. Highway 34, 7 miles west of Interstate 25. Take exit 257B, the same one for the Factory Outlet Stores, go through town past Lake Loveland, and stay left when the road forks. The winery's on your right just past the fork.
Facilities/amenities available: Tasting room and sales area, outdoor picnic tables, parking area, and restrooms.

Driving to Trail Ridge Winery is like stepping back in time, a simpler time when you went to the farm to get eggs, stopped at a roadside stand for cherries, or knew who had grown the biggest watermelon. Look at their sign, A Colorado Farm Winery. You've left the city and its urban sprawl behind and come to the country.

Tim Merrick and his partners bought the farm five years ago from the Mattoon family who had founded it near the turn of the century. The Mattoons brought 30 varieties of apple trees from Missouri and planted them on the farm.

Tim is remodeling the 1913 farmhouse which is now his home, but the seeds of his winemaking career were sown years before. After graduating from the University of Colorado, he lived for several years in San Francisco where he was introduced to "good wine." He lived in the North Beach area and "there was an old guy who lived in an apartment in the basement who made his own wine, including crushing the grapes."

That experience with Zinfandel was the wellspring for 15 years of making wine, a hobby turned vocation. Tim opened North Denver Cellars in 1986 in the Highlands area of Denver, a business that serves beer- and wine-making hobbyists; he even brought in fresh grapes for them. He thought about growing grapes in the Loveland area, deciding that if pie cherries thrived, grapes might also.

Tim and his partners ("I no longer have friends they're all my partners now." he says) bought the farm in 1992, including the house and 8 acres. They have 20 varieties of grapes, mostly French hybrids, including a Norton variety native to the U.S. They're trying to figure out which ones do well here.

"I enjoy all aspects of wine growing, the challenge of each hybrid," Tim says. "They also have aesthetic value."

To hear him talk, you'd never know work is involved. "One of the things I enjoy about small business is relationships with people. We have 50 wholesale accounts and I get to talk to every one. This is a roadside winery. — I get a real charge out of teaching people about wine."

They opened the winery in 1994 with a "custom crush." They didn't have a building the first year so they shared space at the Shadow Mountain Winery in Fort Collins. They were licensed in 1995 and went into full production that year.The first year Trail Ridge concentrated on red wines partly because they take longer to mature and they could give them a year's head start.

Wine is now Tim's business, but he also likes to make sausage and cook. We wondered if soon that hobby might take off and some day we could pick up both sausage and wine there. For the time being, take time to sit for a while on the deck, notice the whimsy of the two spotlighted vines with their "cork mulch," enjoy a little wine and breathe in that country air.

Wine List

Wines	My/Our Ratings
Never Summer White Table Wine	
Colorado Sauvignon Blanc	
Colorado Gewurztraminer	
Colorado Chardonnay	
White Riesling	
Gewurztraminer	
Colorado Cider (7% alcohol)	
Prairie Rose	
Fall River Red	
Colorado Merlot	
Colorado Reserve Merlot	

**Indicates award. Inquire about specific award/vintage at winery.*

Comments/Memories

Roast Leg of Lamb with Greek Herbs

Leg of lamb (5 to 9 lbs.)
6 cloves of garlic, quartered
1 tsp. ground black pepper
1 T. minced fresh rosemary, or 1 1/2 tsp. dried
1 T. minced fresh oregano, or 1 1/2 tsp. dried
1 T. olive oil
2 lemons
1/2 cup Merlot

To prepare:

Make punctures in the roast with a knife and stuff with pieces of garlic. Mix pepper, rosemary, oregano and oil to a paste-like consistency and spread on all sides of the roast. Juice lemons. Pour juice and wine into a clean spray bottle and lightly spray roast with it. Then place leg of lamb on a grill, 6-to-8 inches above a bed of wood coals, maintaining low even heat — even adding small amounts of new wood as needed. Or put roast in a 300 to 325 degree oven. Turn roast every 15 or 20 minutes and spray with more lemon-wine liquid each time. Check for doneness with a meat thermometer. Cooking time approximately 25 minutes per pound.

Serve with a Greek salad, roasted potatoes and roasted, peeled bell peppers drizzled with olive oil, and Merlot.

Shadow Mountain Cellars

Owners: Mark and Lynne Howell
Winemaker: Mark Howell
Year Founded: 1994
Address: 1708 E. Lincoln Ave., Unit 1, Fort Collins, CO 80524
Telephone: 970-493-7345
Tasting room/store hours: No tasting room. Winery produces wine only for distribution, primarily through liquor stores on the northern Front Range and in some Fort Collins restaurants.
Annual production in gallons: 3,500 to 5,000 gallons
Facilities/amenities available: None.

Mark Howell is a professor of microbiology at Colorado State University with a doctorate in biochemistry, which probably gives him a leg up on just about anyone else on the chemistry of winemaking. But there are equal doses of science and art in winemaking, he says, and that's one reason he enjoys it so much.

"What I love about winemaking is that I approach it with a very scientific perspective," he says. "I appreciate that at least half the process is science and the other half is an art form, a chance to be creative. That's what I enjoy about it."

The art of winemaking is in the fine-tuning of various elements that can have an impact on how the finished product tastes, Howell says. There are infinite permutations when you think about things like temperature control, selecting different strains of yeast, measuring and adjusting acidity.

"The art actually begins in the vineyard, with what the grower does to provide the highest quality fruit," he says. "Then it continues in the cellar."

Both Howells lead busy lives — Mark with a full-time job that he loves at CSU, and Lynne with an equally fulfilling job as a rehabilitation therapist. They also have two growing children, so they don't have a lot of time left over for making wine. That's why Shadow Mountain Cellars only makes wine for sale off-premises at liquor stores in cities along the northern Front Range. Howell says they started out giving tours of their winery, wine tastings, and retail sales, but they simply ran out of time for everything. In 1996 they found a distributor and now focus on making the best wine they can.

Like many other commercial winemakers, the Howells got into it as hobbyists — getting to know wines and winemakers when they lived in California.

"In the fall of 1993 we were doing the crush in our basement," he says. "I told Lynne next spring I want to do this commercially ". She said, 'Oh, sure, dear,' figuring it would never happen. That next spring I attended a meeting of the Rocky Mountain Association of Vintners and Viticulturists and introduced myself and talked to them about buying grapes. I got bids on equipment and by August of '94 was making wines."

The first Shadow Mountain Cellars wines were released in 1995, a Sauvignon Blanc and Chardonnay, followed by a Merlot that Howell was especially proud of. He plans to keep those three varietals as his base wines until it's time for expansion.

To try their wines, the best bet is through a liquor store or at one of the Fort Collins restaurants that serve them. Howell suggests the Cuisine! Cuisine! restaurant in this college town.

Pikes Peak Vineyards

Owners: Bruce McLaughlin, John Gray, David Gray, Mike Sinton
Winemakers: Bruce McLaughlin, John Gray, David Gray, Mike Sinton
Year founded: 1981
Address: 3900 Janitell Rd.(some signs read Winery Road), Colorado Springs, CO 80906
Telephone: 719-576-0075
Tasting room/store hours: 12 p.m. to 5 p.m. daily. Restaurant hours: 5 p.m. to 10 p.m. Wednesday through Saturday. Call about Sunday Brunch
Annual production in gallons: 6,000 gallons
Directions: Take I-25 to Colorado Springs, get off at Exit 138, across from the " World Arena," go east on Circle Drive to Janitell Rd., turn right and continue south on Janitell for 1/2 mile to winery road. Look for arrow.
Facilities/amenities: Working winery on a 100-acre estate, tasting/sales room, vineyard, restaurant, nature preserve and trails, abundant wildlife, and amphitheater.

Pikes Peak Winery and Restaurant sits on a 100-acre estate with a long history. It is part of the 1862 Bates ranch homestead, which later became the site of the old Sinton Dairy farm. In fact, the winery/restaurant building was Jim Sinton's home; he restored the original 1880 house in the 50's. The walls were made of cork, keeping the inside of the restaurant/winery will insulated against summer's heat and winter's cold.

You'd think that a piece of land this big would be easily seen from the highway, but the only visible area is an adjoining piece of land which had been sold to the Shriners for their mule barn. You do a little zigging and zagging as you get off the highway through a commercial area, and then, you're in the country!

The first day we went, a cottontail rabbit ambled contentedly across the grass near the parking lot. That same laid-back feeling is evident when you enter the winery and meet any one of its owners. You lose any trepidation you may have felt about winetasting and the snobbery sometimes associated with it. These people like life and what they do.

The place used to have 40 acres of grapes, but they all have been killed by hail. Now they only have 2 acres of an experimental hybrid called Foch (after the French field marshal), so they buy their grapes from growers in Olney Springs, Penrose, and the western slope.

Bruce McLaughlin (see Minturn Cellars) is the primary winemaker, but the influence of John Gray is apparent. John lived and worked in Europe and South America and still travels frequently, which is probably why the wine is unfiltered like many wineries do in Europe.

Everything here is done by hand. Ask for a tour and see the old wine presses and oak barrels. You'll be taken to the basement, which John calls the "bodega" but Bruce calls the "Rowdy Room." Once outside, you can see the amphitheater where the state's first three statewide wine festivals were held. Gov. Roy Romer came to the first, and one of his lieutenant governors attended the next. In fact, there's a letter on the wall inside dated 12/21/87 from the governor congratulating Pikes Peak on the third wine festival.

The restaurant's chef had been Tony Pedrone, who has been a restaurateur/chef for 50 years. Tony moved to Colorado Springs in 1952 from New Orleans, where he had been quite well known; Chef Paul Prudhomme trained under him.

Pikes Peak wine is available in the restaurant. John said, "We don't feel like we're competing with Colorado wines. We want to sell all of them in our restaurant. We've sold in the Bay area and even shipped overseas."

Wine List

Wines	My/Our Comments
Coyote White	
Zeb's Red	
Virgin Blush	
Cabernet Sauvignon*	
Merlot*	
Cabernet Franc	
Chardonnay	
Sauvignon Blanc	
Riesling	

**Indicates award. Inquire about a specific award/vintage at winery.*

Comments/Memories

Barbeque Shrimp New Orleance

By Chef Tony Pedrone

8 lbs. large shrimp
1/2 lb. butter
1 cup olive oil
8 oz. chili sauce
3 T. Worcestershire sauce
2 lemons, sliced
4 cloves of garlic, chopped
3 T. lemon juice
1 T. parsley
2 T. paprika
2 T. oregano
2 T. red pepper
1 T. Tabasco
salt and pepper to taste

Combine all ingredients except shrimp in a large sauce pan over low heat (Alta's note: no particular time was given, just long enough for butter to melt and flavors to meld) and then pour over shrimp. Refrigerate several hours, basting and turning shrimp every 30 minutes. Bake at 300 degrees for 30 minutes, turning shrimp at 10 minute intervals. Serve with French bread to dip in sauce, a green salad, and a white wine like Pikes Peak Sauvignon Blanc. (Alta's note: This is a casual meal ; set out a bowl for shrimp shells and have plenty of napkins.)

Mountain Spirit Winery

Owners: Terry and Michael Barkett
Winemakers: Terry and Michael Barkett
Year Founded: 1995
Address: 15750 County Road 220, Salida, CO, 81201
Telephone: 719-539-1175
Tasting room/store hours: Winery tours and tastings are available 11 a.m. to 5 p.m. Saturday and 12 p.m. to 4 p.m. on Sunday from Memorial Day through Labor Day. Fresh Ideas Gallery and Tasting Room (in Salida) is open 10 a.m. to 5 p.m. Monday through Saturday(134 F Street, Salida, CO 81201; 719-539-7848)
Annual production in gallons: 4,000 gallons
Price range of wines sold at the winery: $6.95 to $12.95
Directions: Winery is located 13 miles west of Salida and 5 miles west of Poncha Springs off U.S. 50, turn onto County Road 220. Watch for sign on U.S. 50. The Fresh Ideas Gallery and Tasting Room is in Salida on the west side of F Street
Facilities/amenities available: A tasting room and small gift shop inside the winery with a beautiful setting outside for special events (description below). The Salida tasting room is in an art gallery that features arts and crafts made by local artisans.

Set along a small stream in a picturesque valley on the east side of Monarch Pass, Mountain Spirit Winery probably has one of the most scenic settings of any winery in the state. The 14,000-foot Collegiate Peaks stretch to the north and the winery is located on an historic homestead with 80-year-old apple trees.

You may want to buy a bottle of Mountain Spirit's wines just for the label, which features a Southwestern-style angel with the wind in her hair. The angel, wearing rose-colored buckskin, is reminiscent of the distinctive "snow angel" found on the east face of Mount Shavano, which is just north of the winery. The beautiful label was designed by Salida artist Pat Oglesby.

To reach the winery off U.S. 50, you turn off on County Road 220 paralleling the highway and then turn through a gate. On the left is the old homestead building (not in use now) and on the right is the apple orchard, with the tree roots sunk in a well-maintained grassy area. The modern winery building is built on the site of an old barn. Next door to it is an old rock smokehouse.

Since Mountain Spirit is one of the state's newest wineries, Mike Barkett, a physician in Salida, was able to research most of the other wineries in Colorado before designing and equipping his own facility in 1995. He or his wife, Terry, a former county commissioner, love to show guests their state-of-the-art equipment. The contractor and crew who built the winery became so interested that they stayed around and were the Barketts' first crush crew (volunteer-friends still help the Barketts crush their grapes, getting some wine and T-shirts in exchange).

If you can, try to schedule a visit to the winery when they are doing one of their special summer or winter events.

In 1997 the winery started hosting a "Mountain Spirit Evening" on several Friday nights that included a cheese tasting, gourmet dinner with live music accompaniment, capped off with a drama/comedy/dance performance by local artists. Tickets to the event, which includes the cheese and dinner and one glass of wine, were $20 per person. You also can buy the wine by the glass or bottle during the evening. You can find out dates by calling the Fresh Ideas Gallery or the winery.

Other special events at the winery include a snowshoe tour and wine tasting in the winter and a wildflower tour and wine tasting in the summer. The Barketts also are considering a harvest party and a barbecue event.

At 8,000 feet elevation, Mountain Spirit is too high and the season too short to grow its own wine grapes, so the grapes and the fruit they use are imported from the Western Slope. The only exceptions are blackberries and raspberries that come from outside the state. The Barketts planted their own chokecherries in 1997 and will use them to make a dessert wine in the future.

They have some unusual wines for you to try, but you'll also find a Merlot, Chardonnay and a Semillon/Chardonnay blend. Try the distinctive Angel Blush (see the recipe below), which combines the flavors of apple, pear and raspberry. Terry recommends the Angel Blush with Mexican food. They also have a Sunrise Blush that is a blend of cherries, raspberries, Riesling and vanilla. As you might guess, the winery's motto is "Quality Wines with a Difference."

Wine List

Wines	My/Our Ratings
Cherry*	
Angel Blush	
Semillon/Chardonnay*	
Chardonnay*	
Merlot	
Sunrise Blush	
Riesling/Chardonnay	
Blackberry/Cabernet	

**Indicates award. Inquire about specific award/vintage at winery.*

Comments/Memories

Chicken Angel Blush

3 chicken breasts, split

1/4 cup Mountain Spirit Angel Blush wine

1/4 cup soy sauce

1/4 cup salad oil

2 T. Water

1 clove garlic, sliced

1 tsp. Ginger

1/4 tsp. Oregano

1 T. Brown sugar

Combine wine with soy sauce, oil, water, garlic, ginger, oregano and brown sugar. Arrange chicken breasts in baking dish, pour wine mixture over top. Cover and bake at 375 degrees about 1 1/2 hours, until chicken is tender. Good served over rice, especially wild rice. Serves 2-3. (Alta's notes: My oven must have been hotter. Try cooking at 350 degrees for one hour and turn the chicken breasts after a half-hour.)

Minturn Cellars

Owners: Bruce and Taffy McLaughlin
Winemaker: Bruce McLaughlin
Year founded: 1990
Address: 107 Williams Street, Minturn, CO 81645
Telephone: 970-827-4065
Tasting room/store hours: 12 p.m. to 5 p.m. every day. It's best to call ahead, but Bruce says if they're not open, just check around at the nearby restaurants or the realty office, someone will be able to open the winery for you.
Annual production in gallons: 2000 gallons
Price range of wines sold at the winery: $10.00 to $22.00
Directions: From I-70, take exit 171, go south on highway 24 for 2 miles, just as you enter Minturn you'll see a restaurant, Chili Willy's, on your right. The winery is directly behind the restaurant.
Facilities/amenities available: Tasting room, deck with outdoor seating. (a restaurant is planned for the future)

Several years had passed since we had been in the old railroad roundhouse town of Minturn. Even though Minturn is in the Vail Valley, its funkiness had made us believe it might have been immune to the change that had overtaken the rest of the resort area. Not so!

There are charming places to stay, a variety of restaurants, new residences, shopping, and, nestled into the hillside, a winery! Minturn Cellars resulted from converting a two-bedroom house with a first floor garage into an operation with a lower-level winemaking area and a wooden staircase leading up the right side of the building to a deck and tasting room. The tasting room's eclectic decor includes wood floors and beams saved from the old house, a small wood bar and tables, Southwestern touches, and antiques.

All this change didn't happen overnight. Bruce McLaughlin's older brother moved to the Vail area in1962, the year the ski resort opened. His younger brother bought the building now housing the winery, and then the family started buying up property before Vail became an "in" place.

Meanwhile, Bruce had started his first winery in 1976 in New Town, Conn., which his daughter now runs. He became an assistant owner and winemaker at Pikes Peak Winery in Colorado Springs, but he always thought about starting his own Colorado winery. He picked Minturn because they owned the property and it was a good tourist draw. As he says, "The skiers and all don't make it to Palisade, but they'll come to Minturn."

If you're lucky, Bruce will be around to regale you with stories from the past or his thoughts about the future. Even with the frustrations of expansion and construction woes, he envisions a new tasting room downstairs, a 110-seat restaurant, bigger decks, and, maybe, a brewery.

Meanwhile he makes wine. "Any time any grower needs to sell grapes, I'll buy them," he says He buys all his grapes in Colorado except the muscat, which comes from Washington state.

If you need a place to stay, he can provide that, too. They also own "Hotel Minturn," a collection of six or seven rooms scattered around their properties.This leaves Taffy in charge of most sales and running the tasting room. She also might part with an antique or two if you ask and the price is right. For now, sit on the deck and drink in the view of Lionshead Mountain — and have a little wine.

Wine List

Wines	My/Our Ratings
Merlot*	
Cabernet Sauvignon	
Shiraz	
Cabernet Franc	
Chardonnay*	
Viognier	
Sauvignon Blanc	
Muscat Blanc	

**Indicates award. Inquire about specific award/vintage at winery.*

Comments/Memories

McLaughlin Family Traditional Christmas Fare

Goose Stuffed with Sausage

1 Goose, 9 to 10 lbs.
10 oz. sweet Italian sausage, skin/casing removed
1 tsp. fresh thyme
1 tsp. juniper berries
3 T. extra virgin olive oil
1 cup dry red wine
salt and freshly ground pepper

Preheat oven to 350 degrees.

Remove liver and gizzard from goose. In a bowl mix sausage and spices well. Use sausage mixture to stuff goose. Truss the goose. Warm the olive oil in a roasting pan over moderate heat. Add goose and brown on all sides—about 10 minutes. Place the pan with goose in it in the oven. Roast about 3 hours, basting occasionally.

Remove goose from the oven and keep warm. Skim off fat from juices. Add wine to pan juices and place pan over moderate heat. Reduce liquids, scraping the bottom of the pan often. Season to taste with salt and pepper.

Serve stuffed goose with Minturn Cellars Shiraz or Cabernet Sauvignon.

Palisade Area Wineries

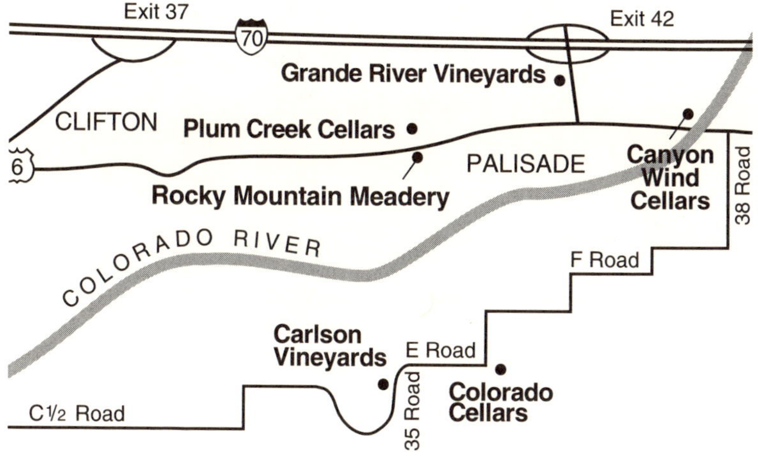

Grande River Vineyards

Owners: Stephen Smith and Sharon Smith
Winemakers: Stephen Smith and Sharon Smith
Year Founded: 1987
Address: P.O. Box 129, Palisade, CO 81526
Telephone: 970-464-5867
Tasting room/store hours: 9 a.m. to 7 p.m. seven days a week
Annual production in gallons: 10,000-15,000 gallons
Price range of wines sold at the winery: $6.99 to $19.99
Directions: From Interstate 70 take Exit 42 (Palisade exit) south and turn right on the first road south of the highway. You can see the winery and its large sign from the highway.
Facilities/amenities available: Well-stocked gift shop and tasting room, public restrooms. Some food for sale, including local bread, wine-by-the-glass sold for picnics outside at one of their many tables.

Any tour of wineries in the Palisade area could easily start or finish at Grande River Vineyards because the winery, its visible sign and California-style building are the easiest to spot and reach for parched motorists driving along Interstate-70. They're also open later than any other winery in the area.

Stephen Smith and Sharon Smith didn't intend to get into the winemaking business when they started out in the mid-80s buying land in the eastern Grand Valley. They knew Colorado's winemaking was a growing business, so they thought they would grow the grapes to supply wineries. They put together 60 acres of vineyards, about half of which are around their winery building.

Grande River does produce more grapes than any other vineyard operation in Colorado — supplying more than half of all the grapes used by the state's wineries. But they also have been making their own wines since 1989, at first renting part of the nearby Plum Creek Winery building and then opening their 9,000 square-foot winery in 1994.

Heavy wood doors with a grape motif mark the entrance to Grande River's two-story winery. Push through the doors and you enter the warmth of the cathedral-ceiling tasting room and gift shop. Outside there is ample room for parking as well as a picnic area. They sell their wine by the glass, as well as the glass if you don't have your own.

The winery itself is built in the midst of about 30 acres of vineyards on a south-facing slope that catches the sun's warmth. The rest of the vineyards are across the Colorado River toward Orchard Mesa.

As an oil and gas landman based in Denver, Stephen had always wanted to get out of the big city and closer to the earth. While in Denver he and Sharon took some wine appreciation classes and started looking around for an opportunity to grow grapes in the Palisade area. Stephen's landman past is not far away even now because his office on the second floor of the winery contains furniture from his old Denver office.

If the winery building looks like it might have been picked up by a helicopter in the Napa Valley and transplanted to the Grand Valley as a small estate winery, that's probably because the Smiths hired then-California architect, Nathan Good, to do just that. "We wanted to capture the winery look so people would know it's a winery," Smith says. Sharon Smith was the interior designer for the winery and also is the wine chemist.

Like many Colorado wineries, Grande River produces such popular wines as merlot and chardonnay, but it also has several unusual offerings that are well worth trying — a Viognier, and both red and white Meritage.

The former (pronounced vee-oh-nyay) is a delicate white wine that comes from the Rhone Valley and entered the Napa Valley in the 1980s, where it has gradually built a small but avid following. Because it is such a rare grape it tends to be more pricey than other varietals (and at $19.99 is the most expensive at Grande River).

Meritage (pronounced like "heritage") is a winemaker's word combining "merit" and "heritage" and is applied to American wines blended exclusively from Bordeaux grape varieties, either white and red. Grande River uses sauvignon blanc and semillion for its Meritage White, and cabernet sauvignon, cabernet franc and merlot for the Meritage Red.

With such a great location along the interstate it's no surprise that about 70 percent of Grande River's sales are at the tasting room, but the winery began statewide distribution in 1996 and can be found in liquor stores in most of Colorado now. And because most of the wineries in the state use some Grande River grapes, you'll find a little of Grande River just about anywhere.

Wine List

Wines	My/Our Ratings
Meritage White*	
Barrel Select Chardonnay*	
Viognier*	
Syrah*	
Merlot*	
Meritage Red*	
Desert Blush*	
Semi-Sweet*	
Late Harvest Semillon*	

** Indicates award. Inquire about specific award/vintage at winery.*

Comments/Memories

Coolest Cucumber Soup

2 cups plain low-fat yogurt

2 cucumbers, peeled and seeded

2 cloves garlic

1T. dill

Place cucumbers and other ingredients in a blender and puree. Chill until cold and serve. Sharon Smith recommends serving it with Grande River Vineyards Semi-sweet wine.

(Alta's note: The raw garlic taste may be too much for some; consider cutting it in half or adding a little fresh lemon juice instead.)

Canyon Wind Cellars

Founded: 1996
Owners: Norm and Ellen Christianson
Winemaker: Robert Pepi
Address: PO Box 1471, Palisade, CO 81526
Telephone: 970-464-0888
Tasting room hours: By appointment
Annual production in gallons: 2,500 gallons (1997 est.)
Price range of wines sold at the winery: N/A
Directions: Approaching Palisade on I-70 from the west take Exit 44, stay right across the bridge for 0.6 mile and winery is on the south side of the road. The Palisade Greenhouse borders the winery property on the west. From Palisade, take 3rd Street east and the winery is three-fourths of a mile from the city limits.
Facilities/amenities available: Large parking area in rural setting. Cool grass under shade tree in front of winery.

Canyon Wind, aptly named for its location at the mouth of Debeque Canyon, is one of Colorado's newest wineries. The stark white winery building is in a lovely rural setting just east of Palisade at the end of a vineyard-lined dirt road.

NormChristianson, a former geologist and thoroughbred horse rancher, has 20 acres of grapes around his winery, principally Chardonnay, Merlot, Cabernet Sauvignon and Cabernet Franc.

Christianson crushed his first grapes in 1996, the same year he built the winery, and bottled his first wines the following year.

There was a great deal of anticipation about Canyon Wind's first wines because Christianson called in noted California winemaker Robert Pepi as the winery's consulting winemaker. The first release in 1997 was a Chardonnay, to be followed in 1998 with his red varietals.

Plum Creek Cellars

Owners: Doug and Sue Phillips, Erik Bruner, Ted Mann and Kathe Gendel
Winemaker: Erik Bruner
Year Founded: 1984
Address: 3708 G Road, Palisade, CO 81526
Telephone: 970-464-7586
Tasting room/store hours: 10 a.m. to 5 p.m. daily, 7 days a week
Annual production in gallons: 18,000-30,000 gallons
Price range of wines sold at the winery: $5.00 to $15.00
Directions: From I-70, take Exit 42 at Palisade south 1/2 mile to G Road , turn right and the winery is a quarter-mile on the right. Look for the 1,200-lb. "Chardonnay Chicken" metal sculpture in front.
Facilities/amenities available: Picnic area with tables, no food, small tasting room and store but plans to expand.

Doug and Sue Phillips and their winemaker at Plum Creek Cellars, Eric Bruner, are among the biggest boosters of Colorado wines and vines. You'll likely spot one of them at just about any gathering where there's an opportunity to promote the state's products. They are tireless advocates of the industry, as well as their own well-regarded wines.

If you want to meet Doug and Sue, go to their winery on the weekend. That's the best time to find them there and not across the Continental Divide at their Denver law practice. Erik Bruner, however, is seldom far from the wines he labors over.

Plum Creek Cellars is as aggressive as any in getting the word out that Colorado wines have come into their own in terms of quality.

Founded in 1984 by a group of wine-tasting friends who wanted to "make their own," Plum Creek has a widening reputation and winemaker Bruner has become a mentor for several of Colorado's wineries.

Bruner and Doug Phillips have been friends nearly 30 years, sharing raft trips down the Colorado River through Grand Canyon and increasingly loving the taste of wine and winemaking. They and some friends launched Plum Creek in 1984, initially housing the winery in a garage at Larkspur, south of Denver near the creek that bears the winery's name. Since their grapes were coming from the Western Slope 240 miles away, they and the other owners decided to move the winery to Palisade in 1990.

Phillips and his wife, Sue, are both practicing attorneys in Denver but still spend a lot of time at the winery or on the road promoting their product. On one trip east in 1997 they found a home for their wine at one of New York City's premier sports bars, Mickey Mantle's.

Phillips credits Bruner's knowledge of winemaking with turning out distinctive wines. The key to wine excellence, he says, is that "you have to have a quality winemaker. It takes work every single day of the year. The wine is ready whenever it is ready, not when you want it to be.(For example,) Redstone Chardonnay is different from a regular chardonnay even though the grapes may be the same. Erik lets the grapes speak to him."

Bruner comes from a family with roots in farming dating to the 1830s. After getting his degree in geological engineering and moving to Colorado in 1970, Bruner started making wines at home. One thing led to another, with Bruner graduating from the Napa Valley School of Cellaring and attending numerous classes at the University of California at Davis. In 1987 Bruner decided to spend all his time making wine.

Phillips, a former Green Beret, also has an agricultural background and earned his love of wine while in college at the University of Utah. His wife, Sue, comes from a family that has lived in Colorado since 1875. She was a copy and news editor at the Denver Post before getting her law degree and is now the winery's general manager.

Plum Creek owns several vineyards near Palisade and Paonia. The latter produces the grapes that go into the Redstone Reserve Chardonnay. At 5,800 feet and 1,000 feet higher than Palisade, the Redstone Vineyard is reputedly the highest in the world growing chardonnay grapes.

Besides chardonnay, Plum Creek is known for its merlot red wines, as well as a half dozen other varietals and blends. In 1996, the winery produced the state's first vintage of Sangiovese, the principal grape of the Italian area of Tuscany which is used so much in Chianti. It also bottled the state's first "Eiswein," a Riesling ice-wine which is naturally sweet because it's made from frozen grapes.

Plum Creek was listed in the Andre Gayot-Gault Millau book, "Guide to the Best Wineries of North America."

When you drive in Plum Creek's entrance, which is across the road from the Rocky Mountain Meadery, notice the distinctive "Chardonnay Chicken" wire sculpture, boasting of wines to" crow about." It was made by a local sculptor. Also take a tour inside the winery and its spotless tanks, but beware of spooking Jack the Cat, a black cat that roams the floor.

Wine List

Wines	My/Our Ratings
Redstone reserve Chardonnay*	
Colorado Chardonnay*	
Whitecliff*	
Festival*	
Redstone reserve Cabernet Sauvignon*	
Cabernet Franc*	
Redstone reserve Merlot*	
Merlot*	
Pinot Noir*	
Palisade Rose*	
Palisade Red*	
Riesling*	
Ice-Wine	
Sangiovese	

**Indicates award. Inquire about specific award/vintage at winery.*

Comments/Memories

Doug's Barbecued Salmon

Fry until crisp 2-3 pieces of bacon per serving. Place salmon fillets or salmon steaks onto heavy aluminum foil. Spread bacon drippings over the salmon; then squeeze part of a lemon over the salmon. Pour 1-cup of Plum Creek Cellars' Colorado Chardonnay over the fish. Finally, sprinkle 2 tablespoons of freshly chopped dill over the fish and the crumbled bacon over the salmon.

Fold the aluminum into a tent over the fish and cook over a medium fire on the barbecue grill. Cook about 15-20 minutes but check every 5 minutes or so for doneness. Do not overcook.

(Alta's note: Could be done in individual packets of 1/3 to 1/2 lbs. fillet each. Would only require a 1/4 cup or less of the Chardonnay in each packet. Good served with a French baguette, corn on the cob and green salad.)

—

Sue's Gazpacho

1 3/4 pound tomatoes, fresh, chopped, or 32-oz. can Italian plum tomatoes, undrained and chopped
3/4 cup green onions, chopped
3/4 cup Plum Creek Cellars' Chardonnay
1 medium cucumber, peeled, seeded and chopped
2 cloves garlic, crushed
3 tbs. red wine vinegar
1 tsp. Worcestershire sauce
1/2 tsp. Tabasco
2 cubes beef bouillon
1 1/2 cups beef broth
16 oz. pitted Kalamata olives, drained and sliced

In a large bowl, combine all ingredients. Cover and chill 24 hours so the flavors marry. Garnish with croutons and chopped chives. This chilled soup is a low-calorie and nutritious start for any meal.

Rocky Mountain Meadery

Founded: 1995
Owners: Connie and Fred Strothman
Mead-maker Fred Strothman
Address: 3701 G Road, Palisade, CO 81526
Phone: 970-464-7899
Tasting room/store hours: 10 a.m. to 5 p.m. daily.
Annual production in gallons: N/A
Price range of meads sold at the meadery: $7.95 to $8.95
Directions: I-70 to Exit 42, about 10 miles east of Grand Junction. Turn right on Elberta Road and travel about 1 mile to third stop, turn right onto Highway 6, travel about one-quarter mile. On the left (south) side of the road look for the gazebo.
Facilities/amenities available: Gazebo (available for picnics and parties), landscaped grounds, picnic area, gift shop featuring wine-related items and gourmet foods, restrooms, ample parking and views of the Grand Mesa and Mt. Garfield, vineyard and orchard for strolling.

Shade trees and an inviting gazebo welcome you to a unique experience at the Rocky Mountain Meadery.

This is one of the few places in the U.S. that makes mead, that ancient and storied nectar of the gods. Owner and winemaker Fred Strothman, who retired from his previous job as a federal administrative law judge in Denver, had to teach himself the intricacies of making honey wine.

When he and his wife, Connie, moved to the Grand Valley in 1994 they thought they would start out by bottling grape wines under their own Confre Cellars label while their grape vines matured. That didn't work out, however, so Strothman decided to make to mead.

Most Americans probably don't know what mead is, let alone have tried it, Strothman admits, but "it sells itself. You just have to get people to try it."

Like so many winemakers, Strothman took a course in winemaking at the University of California at Davis and found out as much information as he could about making mead. "There is no valid literature on mead-making," he says. "We had to try to figure it out ourselves."

Anyone who has tried European meads will be surprised by many of the Meadery's offerings because they so resemble a dry or off-dry wine. In those categories are the King Arthur and Lancelot labels, while the Guinevere is semi-sweet and the Camelot is a sweet, dessert-style mead.

Strothman also has become creative with the remarkable Palisade-area fruit, adding such things as peaches, cherries and apricots to the mead, as well as raspberry and blackberry. In 1997 Strothman took another creative step by producing hard cider.

Strothman seeks quality in whatever undertaking he begins. His 5,000 square-foot steel building is spotless inside and out. He uses a special German-made filter that measures the molecular weight of impurities, removing everything that doesn't satisfy his particular tastes. He searched for the honey with just the taste he wanted, finally finding it in Arizona and California.

"We talk about sterilizing here, not just sanitizing," Strothman says. "The goal is to be like a hospital surgical room, even though that isn't possible."

Step into the Meadery building and you're stepping into Connie Strothman's charming empire, a 1,500 square-foot tasting room/gift shop that feels like home the minute the door shuts behind you. Lace curtains cover the windows and the displays invite inspection. The double doors at the entrance were saved from one of the couple's former homes. The centerpiece of the tasting room is a black walnut counter, made from a piece of wood the Strothman's had been carting around with them for 30 years.

All the items in the store have a fruit, wine or honey connection and most are from Colorado. Sign your name to their mailing list and Connie will ship you one of her periodic newsletters, which usually have several recipes using their meads

Mead List

Traditional Meads | **My/Our Ratings**

*King Arthur
*Lancelot
*Guinevere
*Camelot

Fruit & Honey Blended Meads

Blackberry 'n' Honey
*Cherry 'n' Honey
*Apricots 'n' Honey
*Raspberry 'n' Honey
*Peaches 'n' Honey

After-dinner Series

After Dinner Blackberry
After Dinner Cherry
After Dinner Raspberry

Cider (hard)

Apple Cider
Pear Cider

** Indicates award. Inquire about specific award/vintage at winery.*

Comments/Memories

Chicken Cherryaki

4 servings

4 large boneless, skinless chicken breasts
1 cup Cherries 'n' Honey Wine
1/2 cup soy sauce
2 large cloves garlic, crushed
1 teaspoon sesame oil
1 tablespoon sesame seeds
1 tablespoon butter or margarine
4 green onions, chopped
1 1/2 cups sliced mushrooms
1/2 cup large sweet cherries, fresh or frozen, pitted
1/2 cup sugar snap peas

Rinse chicken and pat dry. Place in 8-inch square glass baking dish. Prepare a marinade in small bowl by combining wine, soy sauce, garlic, sesame oil and sesame seeds. Pour over chicken. Cover and refrigerate eight hours or longer.

One hour before serving, remove chicken from marinade. Reserve. Pour marinade in small saucepan. Bring to a boil and reduce by two-thirds. Preheat gas or charcoal grill, or broil or bake in oven.

Melt butter in small skillet. Add onions and sautÈ 1 minute. Add reduced marinade, mushrooms, cherries and peas. Cook 3 minutes or until vegetables are tender-crisp. Keep warm.

Place chicken on grill and cook 5 minutes on one side. Turn chicken and cook 3-5 minutes more or until just done. Don't overcook. To serve, set chicken on serving platter or plates. Spoon cherry mixture over chicken.

Serve with rice

(Alta's Note: If you prefer less soy flavor, substitute wine for half of the soy sauce called for in the recipe. Use more Bing Cherries to enhance the unique quality of the Cherry 'n' Honey wine.)

Grilled Chicken With Peaches 'n' Honey or Apricot 'n' Honey

Blend 1/2 cup white wine Worcestershire sauce and 1/2 cup Peaches 'n' Honey or Apricot 'n' Honey wine. Marinate chicken overnight or for several hours. Barbecue or broil.

COLORADO
TABLE WINE

Prairie Dog Blush

Carlson Vineyards

Owners: Mary and Parker Carlson
Winemaker: Parker Carlson
Founded: 1988
Address: 461 35 Road, Palisade, CO 81526
Telephone: 970-464-5554
Tasting room/store hours: 11 a.m. to 6 p.m. seven days a week.
Annual production in gallons: 12,000-15,000
Price range of wines sold at the winery: $7.49 to $9.50
Directions: I-70 to Exit 42 at Palisade. From exit drive south (Grande River Vineyards is on southwest corner of the intersection) into Palisade and turn left at 3rd stop sign (Front Street/Hwy 6). As soon as you cross the Colorado River turn right on 38 Rd. (Big sign says "East Orchard Mesa"). Follow that road through eight 90-degree turns or about 5.5 miles while road names change. Winery is on right (west) side of road with sign over the mail box in the shape of a large wine bottle.
Facilities/amenities available: Grass picnic area under shade trees, visitor restrooms, gift shop, tasting room.

Carlson Vineyards is one of Colorado's most distinctive wineries, reflecting the personality and presence of its owners, Parker and Mary Carlson.

One look at their wine list will tell you this is a winery whose owners want to have fun — and want you to have fun, as well. Their labels carry such names as "Tyrannosaurus Red," "Prairie Dog Red," and "Pearadactyl." You may want to buy the wines just for the entertaining labels, featuring wide-eyed prairie dogs and dinosaurs with grapes in their teeth.

Don't let those humorous names throw you off, though. They are part of the charm of this winery, which takes its winemaking very seriously despite the marketing fun. Several of Carlson's wines are award-winners, including the aforementioned critters.

Carlson Vineyards is one of the oldest operating wineries in Colorado, dating to the planting of their first three acres of grapes in 1981 in a former apricot orchard. Carlson, who had made home wine for years, opened his commercial winery in 1988 because his friends convinced him his homemade fruit wines were as good as those in the store.

Carlson probably gets most of the tasting public's attention initially because of his fruit wines — they account for almost half the winery's sales — but you'll find several quality grape wines as well. Above all, the Carlsons aim to produce easygoing wines that go well with friendship and food.

The winery boasts that all of its wines come from 100 percent Colorado grown fruit and grapes and that its fruit wines are made only of the fruit. If the dinosaur and prairie dog names on the labels mystify you, the labels also name the grape varicties that were used.

"I cut my teeth on fruit wines," Parker says. "So when I got into grape wines I wanted to keep the fruit style." As such, the grape wines are noticeably fruity and some are "off-dry."

The Carlsons admit their folksy approach may not encourage the "wine snobs, but that's not the market we are after. If someone comes here with an open mind, they will like it." He wants to keep that Beaujolais touch — wines that are soft and slightly sweet.

To enter the winery, you turn off "35 Road" south of Palisade into a short dirt driveway. The winery's tasting room is in a 1930s fruit packing shed.

Notice the large rock table as you walk into the tasting room. It looks like marble, but is really granite. Put you hand on it and feel the coolness. A lot of people are surprised how cool it is and it becomes an "icebreaker" to help guests lose their nervousness about wine.

Parker, a jovial Santa Claus lookalike without the white hair, is one of the state's best wine ambassadors. "Colorado wines are going to continue to grow," he says. "This is a unique area and the quality of grapes is good."

Wines from Carlson Vineyards and the Plum Creek Winery are gaining notoriety outside the state. The owner of a chain of Wisconsin food stores started selling both in 1997 after the store owner tasted them on a vacation trip. The clincher was an on-board wine-tasting on the Amtrak train to Wisconsin.

Wine List

Wine	My/Our Ratings
Chardonnay*	
Riesling*	
Prairie Dog White*	
Prairie Dog Blush*	
Prairie Dog Red*	
Pinot Noir	
Tyrannosaurus Red*	
Gewurzasaurus*	
Pearadactyl*	
Cherry	
Apricot	
Peach	
Plum*	

**Indicates award. Inquire about specific award/vintage at winery.*

Comments/Memories

Suggestions for Carlson's Vineyards Cherry Wine

Before Dinner

Serve cherry wine with the following appetizers:
smoked salmon, oysters, turkey, or cheese.

After Dinner

Melt your favorite chocolate over low heat and dip the rims of wine glasses in it. Cool slightly in refrigerator or prepare ahead and take glasses out about 30 minutes before serving. Fill with cherry or apricot wine. Sip the wine as it flows over the chocolate. An easy dessert! (Alta's note: I served a few light cookies along with the wine and the addition was well -received.)

Alta's Almost Tropical Salmon

3/4 to 1 lb. salmon fillet
1 lge. banana, cut in 1 inch chunks
2 T. golden raisins
1/4 to 1/2 cup Carlson's apricot wine or other mild fruit wine
2 T. extra light olive oil
pepper and salt , if desired
2 T. toasted, sliced almonds

Spray the center of a large rectangle of heavy-duty foil with cooking spray or use a little oil. Place salmon, skin side down, in the middle of the foil and drizzle oil and wine over it. Put golden raisins and banana chunks on top. Wrap tightly with foil (drugstore wrap) and turn ends of foil up. Place on grill (medium heat) and begin to check for doneness at 10 minutes.

Serve over rice. Spoon some of the juices on the rice. Slip a spatula under meat only, leaving skin on foil. Make sure you have some banana and raisins on top of the salmon. Sprinkle with almonds. Serves two.

Colorado Cellars

Owners: Rick and Padte Turley
Winemaker: Padte Turley
Founded: 1978
Address: 3553 E Road, Palisade, Colorado, 81526
Telephone: 970-464-0574, toll free 1-800-848-2812
Tasting room/store hours: 12 p.m. to 4 p.m., Monday through Saturday, year-round or by appointment
Annual production in gallons: 50,000 gallons
Price range of wines sold at the winery: $7.00 to $15.00
Directions: Take I-70 to Palisade, get off at Exit 42, drive south to 3rd stop sign (Front Street/Highway 6). Turn left and after crossing the Colorado River, turn right on 38 Road. Follow the road through a series of 90-degree turns while road names change. Watch for 35 1/2 Road. Continue south on 35 1/2 Road until it ends at E Road. Instead of turning right on E Road, turn left onto winery's dirt road.
Facilities/amenities available: Tasting room/gift shop, restrooms, outdoor grassy knoll with 10 picnic tables and 2 gazebos, summer concert series run by Sandstone Productions.

Getting to Colorado Cellars is half the fun; you get that Sunday-drive-in-the-country feeling. Then, above the farms and fields, sits Colorado Cellars.

Leaving your car to walk up to the tasting room, you may be escorted by one or both of the owners' sons. As Rick and Padte Turley will tell you, "Here winemaking is a way of life." And everyone in the family works!

Rick and Padte both have business backgrounds in the wine industry. After 8 years working as a retail wine buyer and then as sales manager for two wholesalers, Rick and Padte, who had also been in the retail end, decided they had done everything but produce the wine.

Before buying the winery in 1989, they had grown grapes and sold them to other wineries. The winery began as Colorado Mountain Vineyards in 1978 in Golden and moved to Palisade in 1980. Originally there were 30 investors, but that partnership dissolved in 1986. That November Rick and Padte went into the business whole-heartedly — which is evident in their tasting room.

As you look around the tasting room/gift shop, you'll see Padte's cooking wines, numerous wine-based food items, gift items, and of course, wines to taste. They have displayed their wine awards. They no longer enter competitions, "hav-ing found no correlation between awards won and subsequent wine sales. ... The quality of Colorado Cellar's wines has been well established," Rick says.

Notice the picture of Mt. Crested Butte on one wall. Rick took it and it's the basis for the graphics on their labels. Speaking of labels, asking Padte for a recipe is almost silly. Every one of her cooking wines has serving suggestions and recipes on them. When does she have the time ? The day we were there she was putting labels on bottles and getting ready to go into the vineyards to work. She and Rick are involved in every phase of their business, from the care of the vines to the marketing. Not enough? They also have a lawn and gazebo area available for weddings and concerts.

Wine List

Wines	My/Our Ratings
White Zinfandel*	
Colorado White	
Colorado Red	
Alpenglo Riesling*	
Cabernet Sauvignon*	
Chardonnay*	
Merlot*	
Alpenrose, Rose of Gamay*	
Cherry wine*	
Plum wine*	
Trinity Champagne	
Millennium Port	
Millennium Vintage Port	
Roadkill Red*	

*Indicates award. Inquire about specific award/vintage at winery.

Comments/Memories

From Padte's cooking wine labels

Colorado Chardonnay with parsley, sage, and spices

—Add 1/4 cup to boiling water with lemon juice to steam shrimp, clams, or lobster.

—Mix with grapeseed oil (available in the shop) to baste grilled fish.

—Use it to make a dressing for romaine lettuce, cheese, and mushroom salad.

(*They'll also tell you grapeseed oil is better for you than olive oil and doesn't burn as easily.)

Alta's Italian Brisket

In a large covered pan place the following:

1/2 bottle Colorado Game (Colorado Cellars' cooking wine with Italian spices)

2 lb. beef brisket

Add enough water just to cover brisket

Bake for 3 hours at 325 degrees. Cool and slice thinly across the grain.

May be prepared ahead of time up to this point and kept in the refrigerator.

Italian sauce

In a heavy pan saute 2 cloves of minced garlic and 1/2 of a chopped onion in a little oil until limp.

Add 1/4 cup Italian tomato paste and let it brown

Then add 1 (8 oz. Can) tomato sauce, 1 T. Brown sugar, 1/4 to 1/2 cup of Game, and 1 can beef broth.

Add sliced beef and cook on low heat for 30 to 45 minutes.

Serve sliced as entree with pasta side dish and green salad or as sandwiches on crusty French rolls.

Southwestern Colorado Wineries

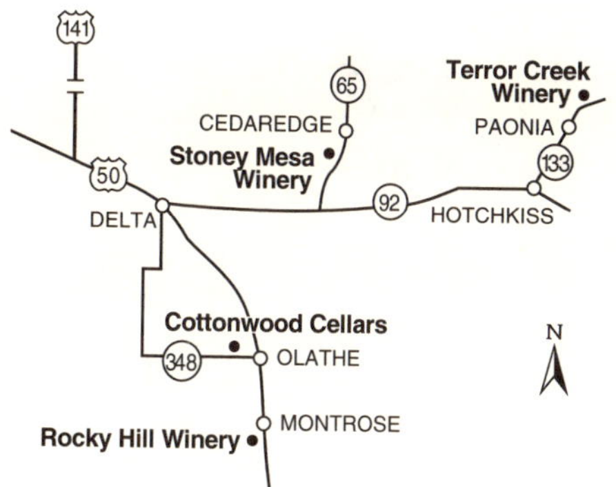

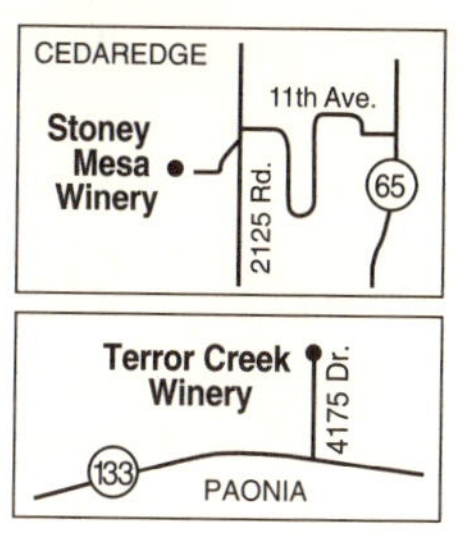

Stoney Mesa Winery

Owners: Ron, Donna, and Bret Neal
Winemaker: Ron Neal
Year Founded: 1990
Address: 1619 2125 Drive, PO Box 966, Cedaredge, CO 81413
Telephone: 970-856-7572
Tasting Room Hours: 5/1 to 9/30, Saturday, Sunday, Monday, Tuesday, & Wednesday, 12:00 p.m. to 5:00 p.m.; 10/1 to 4/30, Saturday & Sunday 12:00 p.m. to 4:00 p.m.
Annual production in gallons: 1,000 to 2,000 gallons
Price range of wines sold at the winery: $7.00 to $15.00
Directions: Look for the signs on the south side of town on Highway 65 (Grand Mesa Scenic Byway). Turn to the west on 11th Avenue and follow it as it curves to a dead-end at 2125 Drive. Turn left and watch for 2125 Drive as it goes up a hill to the right. Follow it up the hill to the winery.
Facilities and amenities available: Free tasting and tours. A wedding and picnic park location is planned in 1998.

Winding through the Grand Mesa on Highway 65 adds to the sense of discovery you feel as you drop into the surprising town of Cedaredge. Surprising because it was new for us and we didn't expect the lovely setting nor the new and ongoing home construction.

Turning onto a dirt road south of town, you zig-zag through a valley and as you come up the hill to the winery, you can understand at least one reason they chose this location — views! The drive into the winery was planned seven years ago when the Neals planted their gewurztraminer grapes.

Although there are 17 acres of land on the mesa above the main vineyard and winery, the Neals planted the 4 acres on the lower level first to establish a vineyard ambience for their customers. The rustic setting includes a small farmhouse, a former garage which has been converted into the red-wine production room because of its 19-inch thick rock walls, the tasting and sales room, and the winemaking area.

While waiting for their grapes to mature, the Neals buy grapes from Grande River Vineyards in Palisade. In the future their grapes will be ready about two weeks later than those in the Grande Valley because of the winery's 5,800-feet elevation. This is not a problem, Bret Neal says, because the grapes should have more fruitiness because of the cooler nights.

Even though Stoney Mesa produced its first wine in 1993, it wasn't for sale. That's because they gave everything away to friends who had helped them plant their vines.

Ron, who travels a lot in his fulltime job as a network computer engineer, grew up in the Granby area but returned to his family's roots when he moved to Cedaredge. His parents are from nearby Hotchkiss and Paonia and Ron said he'd spent his whole life trying to get back. Ron had made home wine, but when he moved to Cedaredge the winemaking hobby just took off..

Ron's son, Bret, joined the operation in 1995 and he and his mother, Donna, took classes to learn how to make wine. The Neals then spent two years learning how to market their products and refining their winemaking skills.

Besides their wines, they have developed a traditional style straight mead made from clover honey. In the future they want to plant cabernet sauvignon vines on the mesa above, where low temperatures are warmer than the first vineyard.

Wine List

Wines	My/Our Ratings
Cabernet Sauvignon	
Gewurztraminer	
Mead	
Merlot	
Riesling	
Semillon	

Comments/Memories

Bret's Quick and Easy Dessert

Chill Mead until it thickens. Pour it over fruit, especially cantaloupe or strawberries. Or pour it over vanilla ice cream. (Alta's note: Don't freeze it ! I tried it and made a mess because the expanding ice-wine popped the cork in the freezer. Try topping that ice cream with fruit and pouring just a little chilled Mead over all. It gives just a light honey flavor.)

Cottonwood Cellars

Owners: Keith and Diana Read

Winemaker: Keith Read

Year founded: 1994

Address: 5482 Highway 348, P.O. Box 940, Olathe, CO 81425

Telephone: 970-323-6224

Tasting room/store hours: 11 a.m. to 6 p.m., Wednesday through Saturday, or by appointment

Annual production in gallons: 3,400 gallons

Price range of wines sold at the winery: $7.00 to $20.00

Directions: Take U.S. 50 to Olathe. At the signal light turn west on Colorado Highway 348; continue for 3.4 miles. Cottonwood Cellars will be on your right.

Facilities/amenities available: Tasting room in the winery building, and you're welcome to picnic under the cottonwood in the front. Plans for the future include a separate storage facility and tasting room, and maybe 3 acres into a wildlife preserve pond. There is also the Westside Gallery Tasting Room at 324 E. Main St. in Montrose.

Diana and Keith Read had dreams of retirement back in the '80s — a piece of land in Colorado — peace and quiet — time to hunt and fish. They found the land they wanted near Olathe and bought it in 1989 as their getaway from the San Francisco Bay Area congestion, where both were computer consultants.

Everything seemed to be going well until they went to a Colorado State University alfalfa conference because Keith thought he might like learning about growing something on his acreage. At a luncheon, the speaker entertained the farmers with a discussion of growing grapes in Colorado and making wine.

"He got me interested in winemaking," Keith recalls. "I said I was going to plant five acres in grapes and everyone started laughing."

So it began. They quit their jobs and sold their home near Martinez in 1993 and moved to this Olathe farm. After reading books from the winemaking institute at the University of California at Davis, Keith apprenticed himself to Erik Bruner at Plum Creek Winery to learn how to make quality wine.

When it came time to plant the seven varieties of grapes on their acreage, many of their neighbors helped out on a volunteer basis. "When you have wine, all of a sudden you have lots of friends."

Their first wines were made from grapes purchased elsewhere in Colorado while they waited for their own vines to mature. They have plenty to keep themselves busy on their 52 acres — 10 in grapes and the rest in beans, corn, and alfalfa. Now their place of rest and relaxation has become a sun-to-sun job.

They built the winery building in the spring of 1994 and have plans to add on a tasting room and storage facility. Presently, customers step into the building, taste wine and also take a tour at the same time.

Ask about their label; they had a local artist, Diana Robertson, do a pen and ink drawing of the spreading cottonwood behind the winery.

Diana said she and Keith have loved Napa wines and they have styled their own to be "real" close to them. Close enough to have their '94 Cabernet Sauvignon Special Reserve be judged as the finest red at the Telluride Wine Festival against the likes of Charles Krug.

Retirement obviously is a long way down the road for Diana and Keith. Meanwhile Diana is known locally as the "wine lady," possibly because of her column in the San Juan Silver Stage newspaper. She manages to write a newsletter called the Cellar Rat and runs the tasting room, too.

When asked what else the future held, Keith said, "I'm going to bring my brother out here and put him to work." At a dinner once, Colorado State University viticulturist Rick Hamman asked Diana what advice she would give to anyone who wanted to start a vineyard. To which she responded: "Go to Europe until it passes."

Wine List

Wines	My/Our Ratings
Chardonnay	
Carneros Chardonnay	
Special Reserve Cabernet Sauvignon*	
Reserve Cabernet Sauvignon	
Reserve Merlot	
Johannisberg Riesling*	
Gewurztraminer	
Pinot Noir Blush	
Sauvignon Blanc	

**Indicates award. Inquire about specific award/vintage at winery.*

Comments/Memories

Diana's Shish-K-Bob

2 lbs. Beef—sirloin or top round (Lamb or venison)
1 T. chopped fresh parsley
1 T. Worcestershire sauce
1/2 cup Colorado Cellars Cabernet Sauvignon or Merlot
1/4 cup olive oil
1/2 tsp. rosemary
1 each red and green bell peppers
1/2 tsp. sage
1 large Spanish onion
1/2 tsp. thyme
12 cherry tomatoes
1 tsp. minced fresh garlic
24 medium fresh mushroom caps
12 long bamboo or metal skewers

Cut meat into 2-inch cubes. Place in large plastic bowl with dry spices. Rub spices into meat; then add dry red wine and Worcestershire sauce. Use cabernet sauvignon for beef or venison. Use merlot for lamb and substitute fresh mint for parsley. Cover with tight lid and place in refrigerator for 2 hours. Remove and add olive oil. Let stand for 5 minutes, but stir several times. Cut bell peppers and onion into 2-inch squares. Alternate meat and vegetables on each skewer, starting and ending with meat. Place a tomato in the middle. Grill on broiler or on barbecue grill. Do not over-cook meat. It should be slightly pink inside.

Serve over fluffy rice with a lettuce or tabouli salad. Fresh baked bread goes well with it.

Terror Creek Winery

Owners: John and Joan Mathewson
Winemaker: Joan Mathewson
Year Founded: 1992
Address: 1750 4175 Drive, Paonia, CO 81428
Telephone: 970-527-3484
Tasting room/store hours: Friday and Saturday from Memorial Day to Labor Day, 11 a.m. to 5 p.m. or by appointment.
Annual production in gallons: 1,000 gallons
Price range of wines sold at the winery: $8.50 to $12.50
Directions: Drive to Paonia on Colorado 133. The winery and vineyards are on the mesa north of Paonia. Colorado 133 doesn't go through Paonia, so start from the stop sign on the highway where the business loop connects with the highway due north of town. Drive east about a half-mile and watch for a dirt road heading north up the mesa (the road is 4175 Drive, marked with a small street sign). The road is just west of a tall metal building on the south of the highway. Drive up 4175 road north as it climbs about two miles. You can see the winery across the vineyards.
Facilities/amenities available: There is a tasting room, but no gift shop or food. Public restrooms available. A picnic area is on the lawn outside.

Terror Creek Winery, named after the stream that washes the face of Garvin Mesa north of Paonia, may be the world's highest winery at 6,400 feet elevation. It also has one of Colorado's best views, looking out over the vineyards, across the North Fork of the Gunnison River Valley below and on to the West Elk Mountains.

The Mathewsons have tables and lawn chairs set up on the cool lawn outside their tasting room that looks across the valley. It's worth coming here just to sit under the aged apricot trees, sipping wine and contemplating Colorado's geography.

Joan Mathewson, the vintner, is the only winemaker in Colorado to be trained in Europe. When her husband was working in the oil and gas business in the Middle East, Joan took several summer "vacations" to work in vineyards in Switzerland and to get her degree in winemaking from a Swiss college. In the process Joan also had to learn French because that's the language the classes were taught in, and she says she still thinks in French when she's making wine.

With that kind of background and the varieties of grapes she can grow at 6,400 feet, it's no wonder that Mathewson specializes in Alsatian-style wines. The cool nights at this elevation help create wines with a real crispness, due to the high natural acidity of the grapes.

The vines she has planted came from France, via Canada and Oregon. In 1997 the Mathewsons planted about 1,400 vines of the Gamay Noir variety, which eventually will go into a blend with their Pinot Noir to produce a Swiss-like red wine.

Park your car at the end of their entrance road, being careful not to block the entrance to the barn, and then walk 50 yards uphill to the winery. You may be greeted by their border collie ,Maggie, although more often in the summer she's comfortably resting in the shade. On the left you'll pass their storage shed, which is connected to the winery by a tunnel built into the hillside. The small winery also is built into the hill, helping give it natural coolness.

Both Mathewsons went to college in Colorado (he at Colorado Mines and she at the former Colorado Women's College), but spent their working lives elsewhere as John traveled the oil-and-gas circuit in the U.S. and other countries. But they kept returning to Colorado on vacations and decided this was where they wanted to live when John retired in 1990. They quickly discovered that retiring into grape-growing and winemaking didn't diminish their workloads.

Wine List

Wine	My/Our Ratings
Dry Riesling	
Gewurztraminer	
Chardonnay	
Pinot Noir	

Comments/Memories

Joan's Sauteéd Steak

5 or 6 oz. Terror Creek Dry Riesling
2 beef filets, 1/2 to 3/4 inch thick
3 T. butter
1 small can mushrooms (drained)
salt, pepper and a touch of garlic
Beef broth

Sauté seasoned steaks in 2 tablespoons of the butter until done to taste. Remove from pan and keep warm.

To same pan add other 1 tablespoon butter, mushrooms and sautÈ lightly. Add Dry Riesling and a bit of beef broth if pan was dry. Reduce and serve over steaks. Good with baked potato and salad of choice. Serve remaining bottle of Terror Creek Dry Riesling with the meal.

(Alta's note: I used sliced, fresh mushrooms and simply sauteed them a little longer. I also substituted boneless loin steak. I used a can of beef broth and the wine to make the reduction which took less than 10 minutes over medium-high heat. This is a gourmet-quickie for those busy days.)

Rocky Hill Winery

Owners: Sharon and David Fansler
Winemakers: Sharon and David Fansler
Year Founded: 1993
Address: 1230 S. Townsend Ave. Montrose, CO 81401
Telephone: 970-249-3765
Tasting room/store hours: 10:00 a.m. to 6:00 p.m. Monday through Saturday, 12:00 to 4:00 p.m. Sunday
Annual production in gallons: 5,200 gallons
Price range of wines sold at the winery: $7.95 to $10.50
Directions: The winery is on U.S. 550, also named Townsend Avenue, on the south side of Montrose. The winery is on the west side of the street across from a Safeway store.
Facilities/amenities available: Parking area with two entrances accommo dating even motor homes, tasting room, gift shop, restrooms and outside deck for picnicking.

It wasn't difficult to spot the blue building with its large mural. There's no pretense here. As owner Dave Fansler says: " We tell the customers, 'You have to have fun or we'll call the deputy sheriff.'"

Fansler will tell you that at the age of Bill Clinton he is second youngest winemaker in the state and perhaps it's that "youthful exuberance" which makes him seem so happy in his latest vocation. He had worked on a farm with his father until 1979, when he got into the restaurant business, an A&W which was on the current winery site. He thought it would be profitable (15,000 cars a day drive by in the summer) and it was, but he was a slave to it.

Fansler still works seven days a week, but says he doesn't notice the hours. Before starting this venture, he and his wife both agreed it would be work, but "fun work."

The Fanslers had always loved wine, first by getting to know Missouri wines and later discovering the quality of California and European wines. They made wine at home and knew that when they had good grapes, they also had good wine. Like so many owners in Colorado, they both took winemaking lessons.

On the thirty acres they own south of Montrose, the Fanslers planted grapes in 1992, but lost them in a 1995 September freeze. Those acres now grow Christmas trees and strawberries, which will be used later for a strawberry wine. Until they buy additional vineyard acreage, they will buy 95 percent of their grapes from Colorado growers, but Dave puts his unique stamp on every wine they produce. In fact, he calls himself "the mad scientist." Try his Ski Bunny Blush or Cherry Wine (a blend of Bing and pie cherries) to get a feel for his concoctions, which might pleasantly surprise your taste buds. The Cherry wine usually sells out in four or five months.

Dave calls Rocky Hill a small micro-winery "where we can do specialty things one year and not the next. For instance, Howling Coyote was only made the first year, but we'll do it again."

The gift shop and sales effort primarily belong to Sharon. Notice the border on the wall and the door to the cellar painted by a local artist, who also was responsible for the mural outside. The Fanslers' lighthearted approach is evident in the door design — the names are those of their grandchildren.

At home, most of the couple's cooking is done by Sharon. When Dave does it, it usually is for contests and events. Hence the award-winning recipe below.

Wine List

Wine	My/Our Ratings
Cherry wine	
San Juan Gold	
Ski Bunny Blush	
Riesling	
Gewurztraminer	
Chardonnay	
Sauvignon Blanc	
Centennial	
Ouray	
Pinot Noir	
Merlot	
Montrose	
Wipe Out White	
Cabernet Franc	
Black Canyon	

Comments/Memories

Dave's Cherry Marinade and Barbecue Sauce

(Winner in the 9th annual Uncompahgre Mountain Cookoff)

Marinade:

1 cup Cherry wine
2 T. Worcestershire sauce

Combine and pour over your choice of red meat. (Alta's note: Dave used buffalo and I followed his lead and used buffalo steaks. Dave gave no amount of time to leave the meat in the marinade, but I let them marinate for about 4 hours in the refrigerator. Without the sauce this leaves a light cherry-Worcestershire taste in the meat.)

Cherry BBQ Sauce

Combine the following:

1 cup Cherry wine
1/2 cup brown sugar
1 tsp. Honey Dijon mustard
1 cup prepared B.B.Q. sauce

Drain marinade from meat and discard. Grill meat, brushing it with BBQ sauce only in the last few minutes. (Alta's note: The sauce is quite liquid, which leaves a mild taste on the meat. To intensify the flavor and thicken the sauce, cook it over low heat for 30 minutes or more. Ribs would be wonderful this way.)

Dave's Cherry Coke with a Zing

Using cherry wine, make ice cubes. Put them in a glass, pour on the coke and enjoy!

Wine Festivals

The festivals listed below are places where you can try Colorado wines, sometimes alongside those from other states. The dates are approximate because most had not been set at press time. Call the listed number for information. Most charge an admission fee.

April

Palisade Peach Blossom Home and Winery Tour, Palisade, mid-April. Call Palisade Chamber of Commerce, 970-464-7458.

May

Taste of the Nation, Coors Field in Denver, on a Sunday in late May, call Volunteers of America, 297-0408. A benefit for VOA, Food Bank of the Rockies, Women's Bean Project, The Gathering Place and Family Tree. Features wines from about 50 wineries, including Colorado.

Winefest, Marriott Hotel, Fort Collins, Friday in late May. Benefiting the Disabled Resource Services Center of Larimer County. Call Supermarket Liquors, 970-221-2428, for information and tickets. About 100 wineries participate, including those from Colorado.

June

Taste of the Summit, Dillon, late June, 970-262-3400 or 970-668-0378. Food, wine and beer.

Wines for Life, Holiday Inn at I-70 and Chambers Road, Aurora, late June. Benefiting the University of Colorado Cancer Center, 303-371-3421 or 303-375-0244. In its 17th year in 1998. Many wines from all over, as well as a wine auction.

Telluride Wine Festival, Telluride, last weekend in June, 800-525-3455 or 970-728-3178. Several Colorado wineries are represented at this festival, which also draws many wineries from other states.

Food & Wine Magazine Classic at Aspen, mid-June, 970-925-6256. More of a focus on food than wine, but there is ample opportunity to taste numerous wines. A few Colorado wineries normally are represented. You'll get to see the movers and shakers in the food world here.

Lower Downtown Beer, Wine and Food Festival, Denver, mid-June, outdoors in the Coors Field south parking lot, 303-458-6685. Features some Colorado wineries along with brew-pubs and microbreweries.

September

Steamboat Vintage Auto Race & Concours d'Elegance, Steamboat Springs, Labor Day weekend, call 970-879-4505. Colorado wineries are featured during the Concours d'Elegance car show.

American Institute of Wine and Food's Colorado Harvest Market, Denver, mid-Sept., 303-333-2378. First annual event in 1997 was at the Wings over the Rockies Museum at the old Lowry Air Force Base. Featuring wines from most Colorado wineries as well as Colorado foods. In 1998, the Harvest Festival will be held in conjunction with the International Gastronomy Conference, which will draw some of the biggest names in the food and wine industry.

Colorado Mountain Winefest, Palisade, 3rd weekend, 970-243-8497. The "showcase" for most Colorado wineries and the first one specifically for the state's wines. Includes music, wine-tasting, tours, food and educational events.

October

Vintners of Colorado Dinner, Hyatt Regency Beaver Creek, mid-Oct., 800-233-1234 or 970-949-1234. A wine-tasting and dinner featuring Colorado wines in a weekend hotel package. Sometimes there is a comparison tasting with wines from other states.

Simplified Glossary of Wine Terms

Acidity. The tartness in a wine due to natural fruit acids. Acidity protects wine from spoilage but also determines its overall taste balance.

Aroma. Fragrance of the wine which comes from the grape used to make it.

Balance. Relationship of alcohol, acid, tannin and flavor of a wine, varying according to its style and origin.

Big. Description of a full-bodied wines with rich flavors.

Body. Fullness of a wine in the mouth.

Bouquet. Smells caused by the barrel or bottle aging, as opposed to "aroma."

Brut. Dry to nearly dry sparkling wine. Has 1.5 percent or less residual sugar.

Crisp. Refers to lively taste of a white wine.

Dry. Normally a wine with less than 0.5 percent residual sugar.

Finish. Sensation of taste and texture as or after swallowing. Often synonymous with "aftertaste."

Fruity. Indicates lots of fruit flavor.

Lively. Usually refers to acidity that gives a positive "zing" to wine.

Nose. Overall smell of a wine, combining aroma and bouquet.

Oaky. The smell and taste, sometimes akin to vanilla, cedar or toasted flavors that come from aging wine in oak barrels.

Robust. A full-bodied wine with an unrefined, rough, texture.

Soft. Describes low level of acid and/or tannin.

Tannin. Chemical from skins and pips of grapes that gives red wine an astringent "puckering" taste.

Additional Comments/Memories

Additional Comments/Memories

Additional Comments/Memories

Additional Comments/Memories

Additional Comments/Memories

Additional Comments/Memories

Additional Comments/Memories

If you have information about the Colorado wine industry and festivals you wish to share with the authors for the next edition, or need additional copies of this book, please write to us at:

Alta and Brad Smith
The Guide to Colorado Wineries
2685 S. Dayton Way #24
Denver, CO 80231